BIG CATS POUNCE!

I0893342

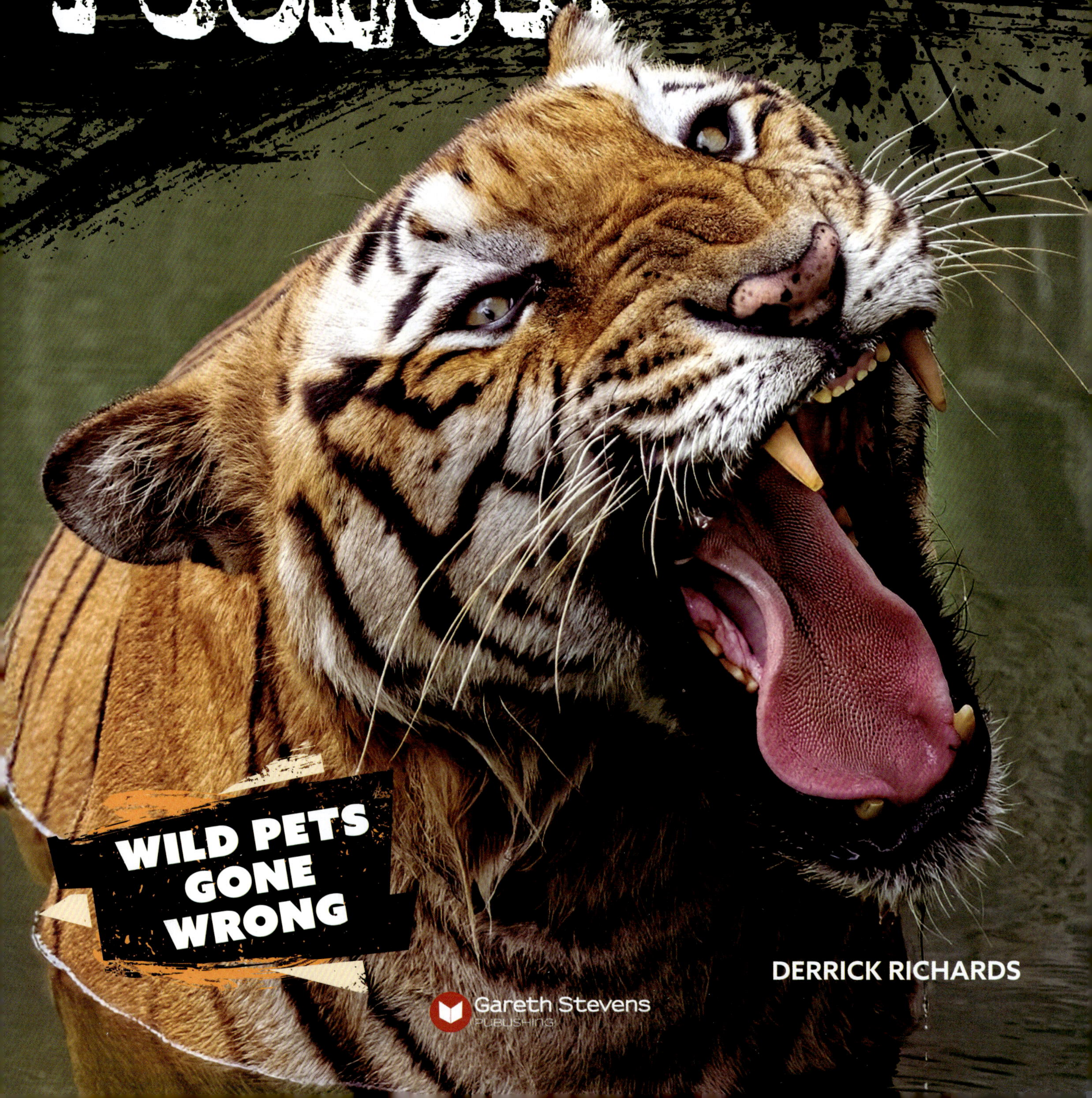

WILD PETS GONE WRONG

DERRICK RICHARDS

Gareth Stevens Publishing

Please visit our website, www.garethstevens.com. For a free color catalog of all our high-quality books, call toll free 1-800-542-2595 or fax 1-877-542-2596

Cataloging-in-Publication Data
Names: Richard, Derrick.
Title: Big cats pounce! / Derrick Richards.
Description: Buffalo, NY : Gareth Stevens Publishing, 2027. | Series: Wild pets gone wrong | Includes glossary and index.
Identifiers: ISBN 9781482479690 (pbk.) | ISBN 9781482479706 (library bound) | ISBN 9781482479713 (ebook)
Subjects: LCSH: Felidae–Juvenile literature. | Wild animals as pets–Juvenile literature.
Classification: LCC QL737.C23 R534 2027 | DDC 599.75–dc23

Portions of this work were originally authored by Julie S. Marzolf and published as *When Pets Attack!: Big Cats are Not Pets!* All new material in this edition is authored by Derrick Richards.

Published in 2027 by
Gareth Stevens Publishing
2544 Clinton Street
Buffalo, NY 14224

Copyright © 2027 Gareth Stevens Publishing

Designer: Beeline Media and Design
Editor: Tricia Hoffman

Photo credits: Cover, p. 1 Wirestock Creators/Shutterstock.com; cover, p. 1 queezz (background texture)/Shutterstock.com; cover, p. 1, 4, 7, 9, 11, 12, 14, 16, 18, 20, 23, 24, 27 ,28 Tartila (sidebar background)/Shutterstock.com; p. 3, 4, 7, 8, 12, 15, 16, 20, 23, 24, 27, 30, 31, 32 Nadia Chi (background texture)/Shutterstock.com; p. 5 Hawatrending/Shutterstock.com; p. 6 Geoffrey Kuchera/Shutterstock.com; p. 8 Tainara Mazzotti/Shutterstock.com; p. 9 Sourabh Bharti/Shutterstock.com; p. 10 pmvtisl/Shutterstock.com; p. 11 Nynke van Holten/Shutterstock.com; p. 12 Ewa Studio/Shutterstock.com; p. 13 Hans Wagemaker/Shutterstock.com; p. 14, 15 slowmotiongli/Shutterstock.com; p. 15 Denis Botarev/Shutterstock.com; p. 17 Krasula/Shutterstock.com; p. 18 Daniele RUSSO/Shutterstock.com; p. 21 Jens Otte/Shutterstock.com; p. 22 Shutterstock AI/Shutterstock.com; p. 24 rblfmr/Shutterstock.com; p. 25 Nick Fox/Shutterstock.com; p. 25 Kit Korzun/Shutterstock.com; p. 26 Anna50/Shutterstock.com; p. 29 schusterbauer.com/Shutterstock.com

All rights reserved. No part of this book may be reproduced in any form without permission in writing from the publisher, except by a reviewer.

Printed in China

CPSIA compliance information: Batch #QS27GS: For further information contact Gareth Stevens, New York, New York at 1-800-542-2595.

Find us on

CONTENTS

Big Cats Are Wild!

Big cats, such as lions and tigers, are fun to see at zoos. They can be very cute, especially when they're young. You might even wish you could have one for a pet. You may dream of cuddling with a tiger cub or riding it around when it's full-grown. You may picture yourself training a huge lion you've cared for since it was born.

In the safety of your imagination, having a big cat as a pet is fun. But in real life, it would be quite different. Big cats are wild and dangerous. They do not make good pets!

WHAT IS A BIG CAT?

The term "big cat" is typically used to refer to tigers, lions, jaguars, leopards, and snow leopards. Some scientists include cheetahs and cougars as well.

Big cat cubs grow very quickly. For example, a lion cub weighs about 2 pounds (0.9 kg) at birth. But by the time it is one year old, it weighs about 100 pounds (45 kg)!

Cougars are sometimes called mountain lions, pumas, or catamounts.

Big Cat Species Over Time

Fossils prove big cats have existed for millions of years. Over time, big cats living in different places changed in body and habits. For example, there are some differences between the lions that live in Africa and those that live in India. Therefore, these two groups are called African lions and Asiatic lions. They're still the same **species**, though.

The tiger and snow leopard are "sister species." This means they used to be the same species in the recent past. The lion, leopard, and jaguar are also closely related but became different species much longer ago.

OLDEST FOSSIL

The skull of *Pantera blytheae*, a species closely related to the snow leopard, is the oldest big cat fossil ever found. It proves that ancient big cats lived nearly six million years ago.

The Biggest Threat

Big cats' greatest enemies aren't other animals—people are. Growing populations of people take land from big cats. This means less space for these animals to hunt, find mates, and have cubs.

People hunt big cats for fur, food, and other animal products. They also take them out of the wild to make them pets. Some people just want big cats because they're exciting animals. Others think they can tame them. Unfortunately, many of these owners are irresponsible, and their actions cost lives. Big cats should not be kept as pets!

THE FOOD CHAIN

Taking animals out of the wild has many effects on other wild animals. The removal of big cats upsets many food chains. Populations of big cat prey may grow too large. Food is taken away from **scavengers** too. Hyenas and vultures are just some of the creatures that eat remains of animals killed by big cats.

If tigers can't find prey in the wild, they might wander into cities looking for food. Because of this, wild animal attacks are increasing. Luckily, tigers are more likely to harm cattle and other animals than people.

Many big cats love to swim. Domestic cats don't even like to take a bath!

The Family Felidae

House cats and big cats both belong to the same group, or family. All members of this animal family, called Felidae, share many features. They have similar bodies. They have claws that **retract** when they're not using them. Felidae have similar behaviors too. For example, most are good climbers. All cats like to stay clean. They use their tongues to clean themselves and each other.

But there are differences too. The most obvious difference between **domestic** cats and big cats is size. Male domestic cats usually weigh less than 15 pounds (7 kg) and can be 28 inches (71 cm) long. A male tiger can weigh 660 pounds (300 kg) and be 10 feet (3 m) long!

HOUSE CATS VS. BIG CATS

Most importantly, especially when choosing a pet, domestic cats don't consider people as a possible meal! Big cats, on the other hand, might do just that.

Time for Lunch

For a house cat, one can of cat food may be enough food for the day. Sometimes, an outdoor cat may hunt mice or small birds.

A big cat, however, needs a lot more food to maintain a healthy diet. Big cats need **nutrients** to stay healthy. For example, taurine is a substance found in animals' bodies that helps maintain eyesight. Animals also need calcium for strong bones. Big cats in the wild eat the bones of their prey to get these nutrients. Bones also act as a toothbrush to clean teeth!

BIG CATS, BIG MEALS

Big cats in **captivity** eat up to 18 pounds (8 kg) of meat a day. That's a lot more than your cat eats!

In the wild, big cats hunt deer, zebra, and other animals.

ON THE HUNT

Many big cats are **ambush** hunters. This means they hide behind trees, tall grass, or any objects that put them out of sight. Like a house cat preparing to **pounce** on a toy, a big cat **crouches** low with its eyes focused on its prey before the attack.

Cheetahs are the fastest animals on land. They can reach speeds of up to 71 miles (114 km) per hour. That's as fast as a car driving on the highway!

Cat Sounds

Pet cats communicate with gentle purrs. When cats are relaxed, they will often purr to show they are happy. They can purr as they breathe in and out. On the other hand, most big cats can only purr when they breathe out. They also make sounds your pet can't—ROAR!

A roar is a message to other animals to keep away. A lion roars to protect its group, its food, and its territory. Some lions roar so loudly, they can be heard 5 miles (8 km) away!

Cheetahs can't roar. They make a lot of other sounds, though. They purr, growl, chirp, and hiss.

Like big cats, house cats scratch too. Pet owners usually keep their cat's claws short. Big cats can have claws as long as 4 inches (10 cm). A big cat can tear an animal apart with its strength! They also use their claws for climbing and marking their territory.

BIG CAT TERRITORIES

Territories are areas of land where big cats find food, mates, and shelter. They are very protective of their territories. If other big cats enter the territory, they can be **aggressive** in defending it.

Tigers have strong jaws filled with 30 big teeth. To eat, these sharp teeth tear meat into bite-sized chunks. Then, the tiger swallows them whole.

BACK TO THE WILD

Endangered big cats living in captivity can sometimes be released back into the wild. However, reintroduction isn't always successful. For example, tigers in the wild fiercely protect their territories. Reintroduced tigers have a hard time adopting a new territory.

Big Cats in Captivity

Big cats need a lot of room to roam. They eat large amounts of meat to stay healthy. And they are big and strong enough to really hurt you! For these reasons, big cats don't make good pets. But some are kept in captivity for good reasons.

Zoos have big cats so that people can learn more about them. Some other organizations keep big cats when they're sick or have been mistreated by private owners or circuses. If the cats are an **endangered** species, like tigers are, taking them out of the wild may be the best way to keep them from dying out completely. Currently, there are more tigers in captivity than in the wild.

Only about 6 percent of tigers in captivity in the United States are at proper zoos. Most are held in peoples' backyards, breeding facilities, or at small theme parks or roadside attractions.

To the Rescue

Some organizations are working to keep big cats away from people. It's safer for people—and the cats! Turpentine Creek Wildlife Refuge in Arkansas is a home for big cats abused by roadside zoos or private owners. In the past 30 years, it has rescued more than 500 animals, including tigers, lions, and cougars.

Tigers for Tomorrow is a **preserve** in Alabama. It is home to more than 175 animals including tigers, lions, leopards, cougars, and other exotic animals. The preserve gives animals space to roam and keeps them well-fed.

SAVING NASHA

Nasha the lioness arrived at The Wildcat Sanctuary in Minnesota in 2025. She had been part of a roadside zoo, where she was stuck in a dirty, dark den for weeks at a time. Now, she has lots of room to roam in her grassy habitat.

Sadly, organizations to help save big cats will continue to be needed as long as big cats are abused as pets and show animals.

The Wizard of Oz *is a fun movie, but it's fictional. Lions in real life aren't as gentle as* The Cowardly Lion. *They don't walk on two legs, either!*

On the Big Screen

Big cats are sometimes seen in movies. Perhaps you've heard of Bagheera in *The Jungle Book* or Aslan in *The Chronicles of Narnia*? These friendly big cats live among people, but they're just characters in works of fiction.

Big cats in movies have been trained for many years. They are often trained from birth by highly qualified trainers. Though these big cats wouldn't know how to live in the wild, they're still wild creatures. People who work with them must always stay alert. Wild animals can be unpredictable.

BIG CATS, BIG MOODS

Many cartoon movies use anthropomorphic characters. This means they make animals act and appear almost human. One example is Simba in Disney's *The Lion King*. Simba can talk, laugh, and act sad. Real big cats show moods through sounds and actions, but they don't express emotions like people do.

Wild At Heart

Many tamed animals have been around humans for years. They will display loving behaviors such as playing, licking, or rubbing up against their owners. This mild part of their nature is just as much a part of them as their fierce side. And unfortunately, there's no way to control which big cat you'll experience: gentle or violent.

Even some of the best animal tamers have been injured by their animals. Big cats are wild animals with wild **instincts**. Even tamed cats can be dangerous if they feel threatened.

TRUE STORY

Roy Horn worked with big cats for more than 40 years. But in 2003, he was attacked by his own tiger. The cat grabbed him by the neck with its powerful teeth. Roy said the tiger didn't mean to hurt him. In fact, it might have tried to pick him up to protect him—as it would a tiger cub! Luckily, Horn survived his injuries.

Big cats can easily hurt people, even if they don't mean to. People should be very careful!

Zoos provide great opportunities to see big cats and other wild animals up close. But remember, the zoo is the animals' home. If you're coming to visit, treat animals with respect!

When Big Cats Attack

In 2025, an animal handler was killed by a tiger during a performance at a big cat preserve in Oklahoma. Police said the tiger attacked unexpectedly, biting the handler around the neck and shoulder. The handler had raised the tiger since it was a cub.

At the San Francisco Zoo, a tiger attacked a zookeeper in 2006. The same tiger attacked again in 2007. The tiger leapt 12 feet (3.7 m) across a ditch to attack a group of people who may have been yelling at her. This time, one person died, and two others were injured. The tiger was killed by police.

RESPECT WILD ANIMALS

Other wild animal attacks in zoos involve people climbing into animal pens. Even in zoos, people need to respect wild animals and their space.

Protect Big Cats

The Animal Welfare Act was created in 1966. It watches over places like zoos and circuses, but it doesn't provide guidelines about private ownership. Something needed to be done to help big cats living in private homes. Even well-meaning owners make mistakes that can cost the lives of people and animals.

Fortunately, the Big Cats and Public Safety Protection Act was signed into law by President Biden in 2022. This law makes it illegal to own big cats as pets. Hopefully this law will protect both big cats and people for years to come.

PROTECT YOURSELF

Cougars can be found in the wild in North America. If you are on a hike, always be aware of possible dangers. Stay close to your guide and obey signs. If you see a cougar, park rangers suggest trying to scare them away by yelling and throwing rocks!

Lion cubs are cute and cuddly. But by the time these big cats are fully grown, they are too strong and dangerous to manage.

Glossary

aggressive: ready to attack

ambush: a surprise attack

captivity: the state of being caged

crouch: to stay close to the ground with legs bent, waiting to spring forward

domestic: tame

endangered: in danger of dying out

instinct: an inborn reaction or behavior that aids in survival

nutrient: something a living thing needs to grow and stay alive

pounce: to jump suddenly toward or onto something

preserve: a place set aside for animals and plants

retract: to draw in

scavenger: an animal that eats the remains of dead animals

species: a group of plants or animals that are all of the same kind

More Information

Books

Andrews, Elizabeth. *Lions.* Pop!, 2024.

Jazynka, Kitson. *Big Cats, Small Cats: 101 Cats You Need to Know!* Penguin Young Readers Licenses, 2025.

Websites

Big Cats
https://kids.nationalgeographic.com/games/quizzes/article/quiz-whiz-big-cats
How much do you know about big cats? Test your knowledge with this fun quiz about some of nature's fiercest felines!

Wild Cats: Big Cats and Small Cats
https://kids.mongabay.com/wild-cats-big-cats-and-small-cats/
Learn about 40 species of wild cats, both big and small!

Publisher's note to educators and parents: *Our editors have carefully reviewed these websites to ensure that they are suitable for students. Many websites change frequently, however, and we cannot guarantee that a site's future contents will continue to meet our high standards of quality and educational value. Be advised that students should be closely supervised whenever they access the Internet.*

Index